In the profundity of Locus, Jason Bayani weaves the [ ] a perfect storm of words, breath, poetry, conscious [ ] "Always I am told I am nothing / and from nothing [ ] so many others in the book resonate to do the work [ ] and race. It is a necessary read for those of us who carry the burden of calling ourselves citizens in the here and now. I celebrate this gift of a book and I celebrate the poet's insistence on belonging.

Truong Tran, author of *dust and conscience*

It seems too easy to describe Locus as a "mixtape" but what better metaphor than a work that draws so much inspiration from Bayani's childhood remembrances of DJ culture? He plays as a selector, where each poem and preface works like a different track to be planned and sequenced in such a way to take the reader on a journey through Bayani's memories and influences. He plays as mood mixer, balancing comedy, tragedy, love, despair so that each new page contains a potential surprise shift to keep the reader off balance yet in key. Most of all, Locus plays as a showcase of how creative expression is not just powerful but pleasurable, where one can marvel at how Bayani's wordplay is filled with cuts, loops, scratches and long, meditative breaks. You reach the end and you find yourself wanting to rewind back to go through it all over again.

Oliver Wang, author of *Legions of Boom:*
Filipino American Mobile DJ Crews of the S.F. Bay Area

Though the Filipino American writer confronts numerous challenges each time he goes to the page (among them, an incalculable range of historical and cultural references, a context of systematic and institutional deletion, the seduction of assimilation by form and language, the temptation of nostalgia), Jason Bayani's poetry collection, Locus, takes all these obstacles head on by way of several strategies—collage, narrative, and mythmaking, but most beautifully and painfully, by examining his own affections, betrayals, desires and fears with all the energy the poet can muster. When they try to tell the story of America in the next century, they will have to recount the violence and the tenderness. Bayani is a poet who longs to gauge both by the honest measure of his one ordinary, complicated, brutal, loving voice. Locus is the place—and the proof.

Patrick Rosal, author of *Brooklyn Antediluvian*

These poems are both poems and tales of magic and myth, "creatures of excess" as the author calls himself. I find this baroque abundance appropriate for such stories of belonging, native land (of the Philippines) and new land. There are also apparitions ("Every few weeks the Virgin Mary statue/ Would appear on our living room mantle"), initiations, and themes of postcolonialism. These threads are woven and meander through the rich quilt. They move in zigzag, non-linearly, with preface in the middle, and more prefaces to crop up later in the book as well. We read: "To know that everything exists in motion / Is to be held in perfect still." That's how I felt reading this book, and that "21 spirits watched over me," as this work carried unique spiritual weight.

Ewa Chrusciel, author of *Of Annunciations*

In reading, one listens as though to an oral history that weaves the story of a country and people, once colonized, and the story of a body, which houses an identity—male, brown, and defiant, recounting and vocalizing a struggle in continuum against the rhythm of early hip hop and of ocean waves hitting starlit tropical shores.

Thi Bui, author of *The Best We Could Do: an Illustrated Memoir*

LOCUS

Also by Jason Bayani

Amulet (Write Bloody Publishing, 2013)

JASON BAYANI
LOCUS

OMNIDAWN PUBLSHING
OAKLAND, CALIFORNIA
2019

Cover art: Rea Lynn de Guzman, "Flashback," 2018.
Image transfer on synthetic organza, 13" x 17"

Cover and interior set in Optima LT Std and Joanna MT Std

Cover and interior design by Gillian Olivia Blythe Hamel

Offset printed in the United States
by Sheridan Books, Chelsea, Michigan
On 55# Glatfelter B19 Antique
Acid Free Archival Quality Recycled Paper

Library of Congress Cataloging-in-Publication Data

Names: Bayani, Jason, author.
Title: Locus / Jason Bayani.
Description: Oakland, California : Omnidawn Publishing, 2019.
Identifiers: LCCN 2018040197 | ISBN 9781632430632 (pbk. : alk. paper)
Classification: LCC PS3602.A984 A6 2019 | DDC 811/.6--dc23
LC record available at https://lccn.loc.gov/2018040197

Published by Omnidawn Publishing, Oakland, California
www.omnidawn.com   (510) 237-5472   (800) 792-4957
10 9 8 7 6 5 4 3 2 1
ISBN: 978-1-63243-063-2

"The existence of a foreign body within another endowed with strength and activity is contrary to all natural and ethical laws. Science teaches us that it is either assimilated, destroys the organism, is eliminated or becomes encysted."

— Jose Rizal

TABLE OF CONTENTS

"How long will this last, this delicious feeling of being alive..."

"I am never home, but I am not lost..."

"Can the subaltern speak?"

"They sleep, we live"

Declaration for the New Year

Let me be   place unmoved,

     what disturbs the water

          a hard humming—which is

the sound

       of memory

            unfurling

in the body—I will not

         let this city

(   )

     I will not stop

        belonging.

"Just clap your hands, everybody / Everybody, come on, clap your hands /
You can ring my bell, everybody / Everybody, come on, ring my bell"

— Joe Bataan

Preface

My older cousin, Sam, rolled with a DJ crew back in the day. We had one of those brick tape recorders and we'd set it next to the speaker while they practiced and when it ran out we hopped over to the backyard to practice breakdancing.

Filipino migration to the US occurred in a series of waves, the most recent following the implementation of the 1965 Immigration Act and an increased need in this country for labor in the nursing and engineering fields. With this influx and with Filipino families beginning to populate areas that were further from longer established community spaces and resources, opportunities to build community came through parties: the house party, the debut, weddings, someone's lola turned 80—all of them prominently featuring a DJ. They gave us the soundtrack, they put us on the dance floor, and even the goth, the punk-rocker, the mod—they all knew the DJ was central to our shared spaces.

When Sam talks about it, he says he didn't think they were doing anything special, he says, "I just wanted to hang out with my friends."

I'm sure when G.C. Coleman laid down those four bars on Amen, Brother, he didn't see 4,000 songs wrapped up inside of it, or what a break would open, what a breakbeat would become.

I want to tell Sam, all those days in the garage, the bumps and bruises, all this survival in America we owe to Black culture—we get to tell that part of the Filipino story.

There are 12 million of us scattered across the globe, two million in this country alone, we know a break well. And someone told us a break could be owned. And we came running.

Transmissions

"Maybe it was my scratching that got those light beams to land, maybe they're
visiting, and maybe I am actually communicating to intergalactic beings"
— Mix Master Mike

To record a piece of music is to render sound
into a three dimensional shape,   a vibration
that moves both laterally and vertically.
It is not a visual language, but a physical one.
When the DJ scratches, it rewrites shape
                                        back into sound,
one alien to our own ears, but a language, nonetheless.
Speaking to higher beings is to traverse the field.

Every few weeks, the Virgin Mary statue
would appear on our living room mantle.
They say you only pray to one God.
In our house there is a God of Mercy,
the one Filipino mothers call Mother,
and mine shows me that to pray is ritual,
each successive Hail Mary running
my fingers across the rosary.
When we speak it is through the beads.

Sometimes I build my god a tower of many failures.
(Don't touch my early 20s, that there is a load bearing wall)
Maybe the reason Babel came so close
to reaching the heavens was not a matter
of height but form, and they made one,
a shape,   of significant volume.

We are always calling,
in some way, to someone
who will listen.

All I've ever asked for
is that you listen.
Are you listening?
Are you listening?

and there is a form

and it matters

who brings it into shape

it must be precise

as if it is made to define

the ways in which a body may enter

as well as how they may leave

if it is not precise

there must be an error

or if not an error

a break in the equation

a hole

and that means

something

had to escape

A Song Reterritorializes

The radio taught me where the song lives in your body. The ways in which a sound draws you back to where the first girl you spent every day thinking about drew a hollow inside of your stomach. The first bellow of a slow jam is never a word, but a vowel, pressed through the throat and emptying out the mouth with such rigid definition.

Youth impresses upon you so much feeling, but gives you barely enough words to compensate for it. Only a song rewound, a chorus on repeat, a kid who got no damn sense of what to do with himself when Janet Jackson starts cooing into your headphones, *"come back to me, I'm begging you, please."*

I can name you every song by every forgotten R&B singer from the 90s that still lives in my body, and this body is a house made of many songs. I got a voice without a lick of range, but this body knows how to sing. Every bit of need and longing in verse, *"...baby won't you stay," "...don't walk away," "...come on go with me, come on over to my place..."*

I recorded slow jams off the radio. It was the repetition I needed, in order to understand where the damage is coming from. How listening to Patti Labelle singing, *"...if you only knew..."* was food. It's continuance was how you filled an empty space. As if singing the things that hurt might keep us alive, a little longer—might make living possible.

On the TV Wesley Snipes is telling Woody Harrelson, "You listen to Jimi, but you don't hear Jimi." Every song I've pored over on every mixtape. Every long night listening to the radio with my fingers readied on the play and record buttons, and I know, therein, something will always escape me. That "ooh" and "oo" that begins every one of these songs I believe is the work of ancestry. I imagine some OG pulling me to the side talking about, "What you know about that right there?" To which I can only reply, "Not enough. But I know it does something to me."

"He who seeks to approach his own buried past must conduct himself like a man digging. Above all, he must not be afraid to return again and again to the same matter; to scatter it as one scatters earth, to turn it over as one turns over soil."

— Walter Benjamin

Tesseract

"The world was always going to be remade by people who were too busy to remake themselves first and who left the world twice as miserable as before."
— Nick Joaquin

*

It was said that in the beginning there was only the sea
and the sky; not a spot of land and only the flying animals
living between. And the waters were quiet. And the skies
were always still. And, yet, everything moves around them,
and there must be something that moves them, too.
When we become aware of our wants, isn't it then
that we understand we are helpless to time? As all things
must be. And this is what stirs the water, and this is how
the sky becomes wind, and when the wind was shook,
it learned to thunder, and then the sea and the sky became
all their wants awakening. How even the sky can deliver water,
even the water can bear the fire, and this is what makes
the land, this is how the gods love. And when the land woke
they whispered to it, the rain, and it has never stopped falling.

**

In time, the wind above the land and the wind
above the sea gave birth to the bamboo.
And the bamboo was strong and it was beautiful.
And because it is both of these, it split itself in two.
And we walked out believing we could only be
one or the other, that we are either strength or beauty,
not that the plant would cleave itself
because it believed we, too, should be both.

—

In another version of the myth (intra-colonial revisionism), the first man and
the first woman give birth to many children (a trait commonly attributed to
the poor and uneducated). They become unruly over time (the Filipino as unruly,
uneducated, and savage justifies their subjection to a more advanced culture) and in his
frustration the first man begins to beat them (normalization of patriarchal
violence) and they scatter in hiding. Those who find the well hidden rooms
in the house are the ones who become the leaders, those who have
hidden in the walls, the slaves (establishment of caste systems as ingrained order).
The ones who hid in the fireplace turn dark and eventually retreat to the
jungle (othering and disenfranchisement of indigenous cultures). And the ones who
escape the house, they are the free men who come back as the white
explorers (glorification of whiteness, reframing the conquerer as savior).

***

The first inhabitants of the Philippines are likely the ancestors of the Aeta people, likely to be the Austronesian seafarers, which gives them a shared lineage with the Aborigines in Australia, and the inhabitants of several islands in the Pacific including Fiji and Vanuatu, among others. Because the Aeta had lived in the mountains they were untouched by Spanish colonization and have been able to preserve their customs and their culture, and this begins to remove them from the Filipino identity. When they lose their homes—because untouched people live in untouched areas that are filled with resources—it's easier to believe this is happening somewhere else. When they start dying, it becomes easier to see it happening to someone else. *What a shame*, you might think. *Them*, that's who the dying happens to—*them*. Though where they reside is within the borders you believe you live in, there, inside, are other borders, and as Anzaldua says, "Borders are set up to define the places that are safe and unsafe, to distinguish us from them."

Ø

They say that when you look up in the sky
you're not only seeing all of the universe,
but all of time as well. The Moon marks
one second behind; Mars, eight minutes;
Saturn, 49—every light is another year past
proceeding to 13.8 billion. I understand best
where I am in the context of a sun
and its orbiting planets, less so within a galaxy,
even less within a cluster.

I was born a Christian, so for me, time starts
            at year zero
and everything before then is another solar system,
another galaxy. The oldest human bones discovered
date back 2.8 million years, the oldest found
in the Philippines is 67,000, the first city
7,400, all of it dwarfing this stretch of time
to which I am adhered. All of it
another light in the sky.

Always I am told I am nothing
                          and from nothing I make myself
                  material
                          Always I am
            told   I am
nothing
                  and from nothing
                  I
                  make
                  myself
            material
Always
      I
            am
                  told
                        I
                              am
                                    nothing
                              and
                        from
                  nothing
            I
      make
myself
                                    material
            Always I am told I am nothing
and from   nothing
            I make myself

                        material
                        material
                        material
                        material
                        material

The Faith Healer

On an Easter Sunday, Magellan ordered mass to be held in Butuan, the first ever to be performed on this land—which makes it the place where Roman Catholicism in the Philippines was born. This is my mother's homeland, one of the earliest ports of trade in the Arkipelago. All ports signal an entry. All that enters, shows you the way to leave.

When my mother took us to her home I caught sick within the first day and it was taking too long for my fever to break. A few days before, we were in Bulacan—on my grandfather's farm—when my uncle started hacking off pieces of sugar cane with his machete. I couldn't stop gnawing on the chutes drawing out the sweet of it, dribbling down my cheek in the sticky air. I have always been a creature of excess, unable to mitigate pleasure. They later found me by the coop throwing up over the chicken feed. Here, in Butuan, my mother holds my head in her lap and asks how I feel. All I can taste is sugar cane, my body recommitting it to memory.

When the fever refused to break, they brought in a healer. His long stringy hair, black wisps in the lamplight. As close to an apparition as I had ever seen. Here I learn there are things you see, but do not say. When we come to the old ways it is in privacy.

The man took his index finger and began to run his nail along my palms. Old language being written. He repeated this, again, against the bottoms of my feet. When he was done, my mother put me to bed. I slept well into the next day. I woke up and all of it was gone, the sick, the taste of sugar cane gone wrong in my stomach.

For the next few days my mother puts the rosary to my palms. I ask her who the man was. All she says is that he is a healer. I am healed, now. And that is what matters.

The Nexus

Every teacher says the same thing. Your boy
wanders. Isn't this true, though,
of every immigrant's child?
No one ever bothers to ask me
what goes through my head.
Honestly, it is nothing, nothing at all
I'm just waiting to see what it becomes.
What if all the difference resided
in something as small as a letter?
As simple as my father's oft mispronunciation
of words.
That when they say "wander,"
he repeats back "wonder," instead.
The delicate matter of direction
that makes me one that runs toward
rather than away from.
Maybe I just make the same mistakes.
The dog howling at the doorway
as I take the last of my belongings
out of the apartment. Maybe
universes do exist in multitudes
and in every one of them
I can no longer see the numbers,
just nameless fragments, a thousand cuts.
Everywhere, I turn the key one last time
and know there is a god in the hollows.
Maybe in every world I find myself
back in the same place. Maybe I always
come home and my father asks
if we can look at the blood moon together,
and I will know then, what I will know
in every timeline. That the universe
is endlessly vast and must be so
to remain unchanged in my eyes. Sometimes
the unpredictable sea is the anchor.
To know that everything exists in motion,
is to be held in perfect still. In time the game slows.
In time, even nothing can be given a name.

A Metric Expansion of Space

> "I told him to put the Philippines on the map of the United States.
> And there they are, and there they will stay while I am president."
> — William Mckinley

Mckinley said he never wanted the Philippines
but they "came to us as a gift from the gods."
Whose god is this, though?
Who are the gods that give so freely
to white men?

Whose god have I prayed to
all these years? The one I am always
asking for mercy. How do I write
my own providence?

They say when the universe expands
there is no exterior space to grow into,
that space, itself, changes.

Nothing into material.

And here I am, what is made to be nothing.
And from nothing, I make myself material.

Tabo

On Tatang's farm, he grabs a bucket of water
and heads to the outhouse at midnight.
The tread of his footsteps slapping
the bucket's fill against the insides;
the way it sways, curling back
into its container. Maybe one of his sons
wakes up. Even the subtlest of sounds:
a violent disruption in all this perfect quiet.
My father is not here. Only the boys
who are old and strong enough
are needed, and there isn't enough to feed them all.
The last boy will go to school. The last boy
will live with his aunt, who has enough
to make sure he's fed.
This is how you start an education.
How you learn to live without attachments.
What you will need to know
to leave the country where you were born.
My grandfather trudges along the night.
An errant drop flies out the backswing
and lands on the dirt, taking with it
only a small container of the moon.
This drop, once whole, once familiar,
having to learn to be something new.
And maybe it thinks, how will I recognize myself?
Who will I be, this far away, from where I was whole.

Preface

During my father's first job interview in the US, the man said nothing and began to look over his resume. Halfway through he kicked his feet on the table and laid them there right in front of my father's face. White men weaponize their comfort. The very ease of it defining the space, the limit of you in this room, the parameters of the field and every inch of it he fills. That chair you're sitting in, that's his. The air you breathe, that's his. Every sound that falls out of your mouth, once it leaves your body, it sits in the room and the room is his. And when you leave, what's left but the memory of how he maps the order of things. How he reminds you that you are impermanent. The manner in which he says, remember, or rather, don't you forget.

you will want | and you will lose
you will want | and you will lose
you will want | and you will lose
you will want | and you will lose
you will want | and you will lose
you will want | and you will lose
you will want | and you will lose
you will want | and you will lose
you will want | and you will lose
you will want | and you will lose
you will want | and you will lose
you will want | and you will lose
you will want | and you will lose
you will want | and you will lose
you will want | and you will lose
you will want | and you will lose
you will want | and you will lose

Freight

When my mother comes to America
she leaves behind my father
and three-year-old brother
to work in a hospital in Richmond, VA
where the only person she knows
is the peace corps volunteer
who stayed with her family
when she was a teenager.

The East Coast is cold during the winter
and there are no blizzards in a rainforest.
The first skill a Filipino learns in America
is how to find warmth.

Back home, the president has consolidated his power
and declared martial law. He says it's for the good
of the country. The communists, he says,
want to kill us. The muslim extremists want to kill us,
and only he knows what's best for these people.

How do you say to your child, we'll see each other
again—hold on, it won't be too long—if you are not
certain. My mother is a woman of great faith.
And great faith is never acquired with ease. Each day
is a mountain, and you carry the weight of distance
behind you.

When my father finally arrives I imagine
this was the first day he could see
his own breath in the air
the day my brother learned
our mother keeps all of her promises.

I thought I was just a block of clay
they found on a Virginia Beach.
They took us across
the whole of the country.
Five days on the road.
There was nothing to discover;
every journey isn't meant
to serve an awakening of ourselves.

We moved to San Francisco
and lived next to the animals at the zoo,
next to an ocean that was the only thing
connecting us to home. One night
my mother opened her stomach
and asked my father to place me there
for safekeeping. Every day they'd coax the fires
in her belly. At night we listened to the songs
of lost creatures. Trying to make a home
among so many living things
that were far from home.

I wonder what it is like to give birth to a child
that will belong to another country. Who becomes
the foreigner, then? Who is truly
displaced?

There is a price to knowing that you are both a thing
that creates and destroys by being. And yet, still,
they will love you. And to be loved
can never be painless.

Coded Language

Dahil sa Iyo, roughly translated, means "Because of You." Few Tagalog songs are more beloved. It's part of a specialized genre of love songs called the kundiman. My parents tell me that one of their favorite versions was sung by Nat King Cole when he visited the Philippines in 1961. In the recording you can hear the audience gasp when he draws out the first *daaaaa* and quivers into the *hhhiiill*, and as he adapts to this new language, more so does the language adapt to his music. It was said afterwards people were calling him the man with the refrigerator in his voice, because when he sang it was effortlessly cool. How effortlessly he understood how to extend into the right notes, to convey every moment of longing and devotion that makes it a true kundiman. During Spanish colonization Filipinos were prevented from outward displays of cultural pride to quell any potential uprisings, so they used the kundiman to express these sentiments, masked their love of their people and their land into songs of devotion to a romantic love. *Dahil sa iyo / nais kong mabuhay*, "because of you, I want to live." In this we know love is both amorous and revolutionary. How easily Nat King Cole dove into this tune, a man who once vocally rebuked attempts by his community to make him take a political stand, who did understand what every person of color who makes art in America comes to know. Our bodies are politicized and so will be everything these bodies make. Even in a love song you have no escape.

The Low Lands

In my grandfather's last days
he wandered the rice fields alone.
What was left of his mind bringing him back
to what he spent his entire life building.

We are the land—lupa ay buhay, land is living.

When my father talks of his poverty, he presents
a bowl of rice and says, "Your Inang
would put one piece of fish on the table,
and we would press our fingers
against it for flavor." Mimicking his hand
scooping rice out of the bowl.

Inside the home he makes halfway across the world,
he assures us we will never run out.

The rice is our land,
and if we have the rice
it means we are living.

In Tacloban, eight people die raiding a warehouse
that doesn't exist on any maps. They were crushed
by a collapsing wall while the typhoon's survivors
carried out 33,000 bags of rice around them.

There is enough in this country to feed every citizen.
But food is a generative property. It presents value,
and value is a curious thing. Every number
in an economic equation is tied to a life.
And the loss of it becomes an economic decision.

The sound of dry grains, or rice washing in the pot,
those are places where my father lives.
Both the satisfaction of feeding his family
and the worry we will go hungry
as he once was. Sometimes

more of it the worry. I often forget
that we were rice farmers
and that the value of us
is tied so intimately to a simple grain.

There are warehouses filled with rice,
in case of an emergency, and the poor
are always expected
to become accustomed
to emergency.

When the waters come, again,
what will happen when the doors do not open?
The doors. The doors are a made thing.
We are the land. *Lupa ay buhay*. Land is living.
The rice has always been ours to begin with.

"... I return to scenes within the U.S. colonial archive to trace a different genealogy of Filipino listening, a disobedient one that allows us to hear tropical renditions"

— Christine Bacareza Balance

Preface

Around 1980 my parents bought a home in Fremont, CA. About 30 miles south of San Francisco. We were the first Filipino family on our block, then my godparents moved next door, and my cousin down the street. I used to tag along with my my brother and older cousins, we'd ride our bikes all around the neighborhood, and found every other Filipino kid that moved in.

We used to hang out at my cousin's house. One day, one of the kids couldn't stop talking about this breakdancing movie that was out at the theater, and my brother and I ran home to beg our mom to take all of us there. We used to have one of those Vanagons, like the Scooby Doo Mystery Mobile. She piled all of us in and drove us over to see Beat Street down at the Cinedome. That scene where Rocksteady Crew and New York City Breakers started battling had us losing our minds. We couldn't stop slapping at each other, pointing at the screen, *did you see that!?* This is what the body can do... this is what black and brown bodies can do—defy gravity. At the end of the movie, after Kenny K eulogizes Ramo in verse, Melle Mel hits the mic and drops these bars:

Dachau, Auschwitz, Hiroshima
Vietnam, Leningrad, Iwo Jima
Okinawa, Korea, THE PHILIPPINES
Devastation, death, catch the killing machine

I tugged on my brother's shirt, *Did you hear him? He said the Philippines!*
You listen to the whole song, he was rapping about the futility of war, imperialism, how capitalism inevitably leads to this. I was eight, I wasn't getting any of that, I just heard *Philippines*. As if hearing this made our homeland real in this country, which in turn would mean I exist here as well. Often I felt as if I didn't.

But there was a message, something about where the lines are drawn, and he's telling you which side you're likely to fall on.

We Go Boom

The neighbors ask why all the Filipino kids
are in the streets dancing to rap music.
Maybe it's because the ocean works on a continuous rhythm
and we like continuous rhythms.
Because language is meant to slap and swoon
and so are our bodies.
Because we ain't trying to give a fuck
about some REO Speedwagon.
Because we walk out our doors and don't come home
until the streetlights are on.
Because we have a surplus of cardboard boxes.
Because Fisher Price makes turntables for children.
Because we don't own clubs or discos or bars
so we purchase lights and sound systems, build our own
rigs and tables and walk into our garages
hang up a strobe light and say
"this is a nightclub."

Because we have a flair for the dramatics.
Because we often become
what we're told we shouldn't be.

Because we stepped foot on this land
before the first English settlement.
Because this country can't imagine
a labor class without dark-skinned bodies.
Because we walked with the UFW
but keep getting treated
like we were accidentally caught in the picture.
Because we been around hip-hop since the beginning
but keep getting treated
like we were accidentally caught in the picture.
(Filipinos: photobombing American history for hella long).

Because the music is loud and aggressive and it thumps.
Because we are loud and aggressive and we thump.
Because Joe Bataan recorded Rap-o-clap-o in 1980
Because our parents are listening
to James Taylor and Eddie Money.
Because we ain't stepping off this cardboard
until someone gets one full rotation off their head.

Because all the gangsters dance to it, and the only
cool Filipinos older than us are all the gangsters.
Because that lean we got, the curl of our lips,
how we learned the language of defiance in America,
we owe to black culture

Because so many of our prisoners are political prisoners.
So many of our dead are political deaths.
Because we can bounce to this, just differently.
Because it makes us bounce.
Because even as we get older,
and the body don't work the way it used to,
when the first charge of the boom bap starts playing,
watch our smiles grow boldly arrogant.
Watch our palms start waving the sky down.

Into the Empty Field

My mother sends me to the neighbors
so she can get enough sleep
before the next night shift at the hospital.
Their lola watches over me,
unable to speak a word of English.
I get used to the slight variances in meaning
when she talks, the way she shoots a "pssst"
through her teeth, and how to follow the directions
of her pointed lips.

Outside our block is an empty field
they're clearing for homes,
we spend the summer chasing jackrabbits there
and building forts from spare pieces of wood we found
at the construction sites. My older brother believes
we can take this place for ourselves,
when we can get on our bikes
we write our own maps inside of this country.

Every day during summer, we sit under the railroad tracks.
Every train passing over head, a song of the world
crashing in.

At 3:30 is when my brother comes to pick me up.
That I can depend on seeing him shuffling down the street,
his fingers running up and down his backpack straps
and that he can see me, sitting on the porch to meet him
is how we learn to trust those closest to us.

Everywhere around us is becoming strip malls
and tract housing and all the jackrabbits
are disappearing. At the park
my brother takes a bloody nose
standing between me and a white kid's fist.

What happens when there is nothing left to discover?
When did we become such directionless things?

Tonight I wake up from another bad dream.
In it, I'm older, a grown man walking out
of the county jail. My brother
is the first person I call.
When I tell him where I am, he breaks down
and says he knows he hasn't been there for me.
He won't stop telling me he's sorry.

I want to wake my brother, in the bunk below
and tell him, "Everything wrong with me, isn't your fault.
You just outgrow everything before me."

I want to say, "all my life I'll think of you
whenever I see an empty street or sit inside
or an open field. And I'll think, it's almost 3:30,
he'll be coming for me soon.
He'll show me the way home."

When You Tell a Boy

The kids who beat me never hit me
in the face. It's as if all I learned was to hide
the terrible things happening between us.
I know the dense sound of knuckle
popping the fabric. The sound drops me with it.

I know where you can hit a person
in the chest to take the breath from them.
You take the breath, you take the heart.
And that's what they say when a kid gets beat down,
I *snatched that fool's heart,*

the pride in which you can declare
how you make another boy into a loveless thing.

The first time I ever beat another kid,
I slammed his head to the ground while I was crying for my mother.
I never fought because I am the toughest person in the room.
I've only fought because I had nowhere else to put it.

To live with violence is to not know how to live without it.
Maybe that is what a curse really is.
That I would wish something so terrible upon you as a cycle repeating.

When I was a kid they used to make me clean the chalk boards.
It was the quietest part of my day. I'd be alone long enough
I'd start playing with the muck between my fingers.
The dirt of me is the dirt of me. I got an anger
that puts the worry to my bones.

If I was truly honest I would say I wish I could know what it is like
to be touched without recoiling. That I could tell someone
they are beautiful or hear them
tell me the same without flinching.

21 Spirits

1.

"Brother, might is our immense mother,"
Li Young Lee wrote in my book 15 years ago.

(To be honest, I didn't know what the fuck he was talking about, but I
was playing like I did)

Maybe it's how I can say violence cradles us
and know you'd get what I mean.
The odd comfort of a clenched fist,
how we look for the seam in stone.

I have tried to make a life of poetics, Jon,
and I don't see a seam, just a brick.

We break shit with heavy objects.
That is what we do when you put it in our hands.

2.

The mystic took one look at you and said,
"This one! This one has 21 spirits watching over him."
And I wonder if they have been watching me, too.
If they've been there for every single mistake.
                              If every time I fall,
they could only watch me pass through
the impossible cushion of their arms.

3.

Do they only show themselves to you, because I am too afraid?

They don't make this world for people who see like you do.

What if I'm just too fond of this awful world.
What if this, alone,
                    is too much to bear, already.

4.

Maybe if I say enough, I'll get to become a memory
inside of someone else. Maybe they'll care for me better
than I've ever cared for myself. Maybe they'll say my name
back to me, and it is with all of the tenderness I have tried to learn
and failed at learning. Maybe there will still be time to become
something newer, that time isn't escaping it's just shifting
the lens a little. I am much more mortal than I was the day before.
                    I'd like to be a thought someday. A heavy one.
Something that gets slapped on the table and shudders the body of
whoever it gets laid in front of.

5.

A year ago we climbed a church tower in Zurich, Switzerland and
watched the city rusting under the frost. You had asked me how I was
doing. Which meant you were asking me about her. I told you I was
good and the city looks beautiful from up here. I imagine she'd say how
typical it would be of us Bayani men, to be so unwilling to communicate
completely. She's not wrong. I don't miss her. I miss being in love and I
mistake that feeling for her sometimes.

6.

Maybe grief is not a singular emotion, but a system,
not felt, but experienced—we are beheld.

7.

I remember one summer Ma forgot to pick you up
from basketball practice.
When we pulled up to the school, you came running at the car
like you were sure you'd be lost forever. You taught me
how long time feels when you are afraid.
How slow it is when you are alone. I promised then
I'd make sure you'd never feel abandoned again.
But when that boy gave you your first hit of crack
I was somewhere else.

8.

When you were three, one of our uncles in the Philippines kept calling to let us know *Tatang* had passed away. I couldn't understand what he was saying so I kept hanging up the phone. When you were a baby you got used to *Inang* speaking to you in Tagalog, the slow percussion of her speech. It is inherent in you, the words. All I got is my skin. That's what I live with. This and everything it carries.

9.

You said the ghosts would haunt you at night.
I don't believe in these things, but I believe you.

10.

Everywhere you go across the world,
picking up new spirits.
a creeping shadow from Tokyo,
a wailing noise from Instanbul.
Sometimes, you tell me, it is Inang's hand that wakes you.
You know this because when you were a kid
she would run the back of her knuckles over your spine
as you slept.

11.

I tell you that I know she watches me too
and I am afraid one day I will see her.
You tell me I can ask her to leave me alone.
But Jon, I don't want her to ...

12.

It was an overhand right. I set it up with a few jabs to the body. Had to switch up my stance because you favor kicks with your right leg and kept nailing me on the inside. I hit you in the shoulder and felt my wrist crumple on impact. I hit you hard enough to send you reeling towards the floor. My wrist, it still ain't right. It was all worth it. I'd do it again.

13.

How many times
they looked at us
and saw trouble,
when all we wanted
was a comfort
in this place
they did not believe
we had a right
to be given.

14.

If ever I get old enough for a cane, I'm gonna hit you with that cane. I'm not trying to get healthier, I'm just trying to get old enough to fight you as a senior citizen.

15.

I'm pretty sure I can still kick your ass. You workout every day of the week and have practiced Muay Thai for five years. All I got are the poems I've written and the 8 hours of gym time I barely fit into the week, but when you come home you want to drink wine with me and it makes me want to punch you in the face.

16.

I tried looking up whether or not two brothers had ever fought each other in boxing. As far as I know it's officially happened twice, in 1993. Marty vs Eric Jubowski and Kusuo vs Katsuaki Eguchi.

Both fights ended in a knockout. The Klitschko brothers said they sparred once and one of them left with a permanent scar on his face and the other, a broken leg.

17.

Everyone I've ever punched in the face looked like me.
I swung at a white kid once and missed.

(that has to mean something, doesn't it?)

18.

Maybe they watch us and say,
"look at you, the only people
you can really hurt is each other."
Doesn't that feel like a home?

19.

Often there is a person
trying to tell me something
in the machine of them
is broken,

and what I hear is them telling me
something in the machine
of you will be broken, too.

20.

All I see is the mess,
instead of everything
that has withstood.

21.

I know of no home other than memory.
This wreckage we make wears both our names.
Ain't no place out here know how to hold us,
the wild noise in our bodies that summons the dead,
this divine armor, this mighty mother.

I'd like to be a thought someday. A heavy one. Something that gets slapped on the table and shudders the body of whoever it gets laid in front of. I'd

be a thought ████ . ████ one. ████ that ████

████ shudders ████ ████ . I'd

like to ████ slap

the table ████ the body ████ . I'd ██

██ be ████ someday. A ███ one. Something ████ the

table ████ the body ████ laid ████ . I'd

be a ████ heavy one. ████ that gets ████ on the

table and shudders ████ I'd

be ████ Something that gets

████ the body ████ . I'd like to

be a ████ thing ████ lapped ████

████ and ████ the body of who███ gets ████ . I'd like to

be a thought someday. ████ Something ████ the

████ shudder█ the body ████ it gets ██ in front of. ████

be ████ someday. █ heavy ████ me ████ on the

████ body ████ laid ████ . I'd ██ to

█ a █ought so███ day. █ heavy on████ that ██ slapped on █

█able a███ udder████ of █ ever it ████ in ██ of. I'd like to

be a thought someday. A heavy one. Something that gets slapped on the table and shudders the body of whoever it gets laid in front of.

My Homie's Car Still Had an 8-track in It

track 3: Under the Streetlamp by Joe Bataan

There is no name for being young and without direction in
a rudderless city. To count time under every different street
light where you dreamt about girls and places that didn't look
like here. This is what hanging with the fellas means when
you're young. A place to bide time until you figure out how
the body works. Or somewhere to crash into, during all the waiting.

just dreaming of the days that lie ahead
and growing up was the one dream that was in our heads

It felt like every day was looking for somewhere to go. So much
quiet we were trying to fill through car stereos and boom boxes.
One of the girls we rolled with flashed me in the back seat one night.
Caught only a glimpse of her nipple in a passing switch of moon.
We just kept driving like we always do, and when she got tired she leaned
her head against me. Her lipstick smudged on my shirt.

just dreaming of the days that lie ahead
and growing up was the one dream that was in our heads

Before I left town my homegirl called me to pick her up. Figured
there was trouble with her boyfriend, again. When she got in my car
her guy was standing at his doorway, looking like he was ready
to spit my name out of his mouth. Watched him throw up his set
while we drove off. She sat there quiet, looking down at her hand,
lightly pressed against her stomach. "I got an abortion, Jay"
is what she told me. All I could do was grip the steering wheel
and drive off. I told her I'd bring her home, but I meant to say,
"Anywhere you want to be, I'll take you. Anywhere you want to go."

just dreaming of the days that lie ahead
and growing up was the one dream that was in our heads

On Color

My auntie asks why I'm so dark,
the word locking her face
into a mild look of disgust.
She leans into it, a reminder,
this is the order of values
and everyone knows their place.

When I'm alone, I imagine a place,
one that doesn't soften me in the dark
there in the order of values.
I am learning to love my own face,
how you fortify a memory,
how you quiet the disgust.

There is nothing left discussed.
I know this is my place.
I know it's always a warning.
I know what it means to be dark.
I know this won't change, my face.
I know my value

and what is disposed. I value
everything left behind in disgust,
everything they wrote on my face.
There is no permanence to place.
Everywhere for me is unfamiliar dark,
a body rendered into remembrance.

Every boy who beat me is a souvenir,
every bit of me broken of value,
every time I ached to scrub the skin of its dark.
I grow rubies out this disgust.
I terraform that shit to make a place
and cup these god hands against my face.

When I'm alone, I trace the contours of my face.
How I come back to this body is ritual,
how I believe, I am a more resilient place
Everything I am, is earned value.
I tell my homies with feigned disgust,
I'm so sick with it, I got that original skin.

Maybe all I'm meant to be is an errant dark,
some monument to a god of disgust,
a quiet place of disjunctive values.

"How long will this last, this delicious feeling of being alive..."

— Alexander Shulgin

Preface

Some of the earliest mixes we got from my cousin's crew were all electro and freestyle: Newcleus, Egyptian Lover, Trinere, Shannon—that rapid percussion of the TR-808 always texturing the background. When I started listening to house and drum n' bass that shit felt like home to me. Every bit of music I listen to shares DNA. It shares history. In the 60s and 70s, people of color and queer folks start dancing and they raid nightclubs, blow up records at Comiskey Park. They try to dead it, more music pops up in its place. Disco goes, but it just becomes house in Chicago, freestyle in the Latinx clubs in New York. I've always been following this music. I spent more time at clubs than I did in school. The first time my friend gives me ecstacy I tell her, I ain't ever felt this free, or maybe, this is what free people must feel.

In 1912, Anton Kollisch first synthesized MDMA. A by-product of his work developing a more effective blood clot agent. Happy accidents. Everything that gets you fucked up was probably made by a happy accident. Then in the 70s some hippie scientist, named Alexander Shulgin synthesized the kind of MDMA that was popularized as a party drug.

I know what this body is when it is consumed by happiness. What's ever gonna match up? In my most trying hours I yell out that man's name, "Alexander Shulgin!" And all I really want is for a white man to shoulder the weight of my responsibilities. But it felt good. That good don't ever leave you. And you keep trying to find that good somewhere else. And it ain't ever the same song. And still you keep humming along to it.

How Leaving Your Drugs is Like Leaving Your Lover

It gone bad long ago,
nobody talks about it.
Or she would, but you can't
stop looking up at the stars.
In there, you say is a center
from which all points manifest.
The Archimedean spire
of the universe.
All points hold
the lines to form,
You tell her, we return
to these lines, newer,
better, more complete
than we were before.
And there she sees
the boy who wore
the stars underneath
his skin. Who desires
the impossible task
of everything. And each day
you reach out into the entirety
you make her a smaller point
that takes you further still.
And always she pulls you back
and you are her best memory, again,
until there are no more good memories left.
And still she believes one day
you will return newer, better,
more complete than you were before.
And then you say, "Look up there,
at what I have drawn only for you."
And it is a beautiful thing, isn't it?
But all she sees is an endless wheel.
All she sees, a circle that never closes.

All of Memory Becomes Myth in the End

Long and far from the old city. Everyone above the wild stalk.
We wild and weightless. Our bodies named and named, again.
We float until the sun comes up, we float until the next bar opens
at 6am. We float, again. We fall into the cradle of each other,
with enough music to last us to rest. We fall apart; we fall, apart.
We soften the drums a little. We lower the bass. We got jobs,
we rise early. We pay bills on time. We matrimony. We
fail. We learn the new gravity. We go heavy across the pavement.
We don't dance so good, anymore. Maybe once in a while
we find our legs. We try—we try, again. We accumulate
the bills, books, new ailments, regrets. We GO to clubs
to watch other people dancing. We listen to clothes in the dryer,
loose fan knocking on rotation. We lose our CDs.
Where is the old city, now? The morning orange, and silken.
The body, alight. We float. The body an empty cup.

This is Me in Adult Clothes

Traffic is like being ferried along a calm and gentle river
that hates you. It hates you so hard you skip hating it back
and just move on to other people.

Maybe it's the smell of coffee or how the mug got a busted button
so I gotta keep jiggling it to close off the spout
but I know myself by routines.
I recognize myself by the actions I can't stop repeating.

In my dreams I am unpredictable. But ask anyone
who has ever loved me. And they will tell you
I eventually do everything they expected.
I am alone now. I have fulfilled many lowered expectations.

I'm in a box, surrounded by other boxes. Moving my box
alongside their boxes. The woman next to me wants to burst out
singing. We all know it. Everyone sneaks a look at her
harnessing grand gestures in tiny movements.
I'm wiping glitter off the microphone, too, here.
Paid extra for the spoiler on my back trunk
because I wanted my box to be a little more special.
I'm just trying to get where money is and bring it back
to where money goes away.

Sometimes I go places where I can feel special
or watch other people be special. At night
I'm a different animal than this. During the day
I get really excited because I got to the tenth coffee
and the tenth coffee on my punch card means next one is free.

And all this drudgery and sameness and it's ok, I say.
I want to yell out to the woman
who dreams of dancing with somebody
who wants to feel the heat with somebody
that we are on a planet that is spinning
1,000 miles per hour and that moves
through space about 67 times faster than that.
"We're going places, me and you,
just you wait and see."

In the end we found out the roads
had been blocked off because a man
who was holding onto the undercarriage
of a semi-truck eventually fell off
and was torn to pieces on the freeway.
Nobody knew what they had hit.
It was dark and some of the drivers
came home to find pieces of him
stuck to their cars. The story was
he approached a sleeping driver
in Berkeley and hassled him for a ride.
The driver refused so he hid under the trailer
and waited for him to leave. He made
it 20 miles, all of the morning cold rushing
right into him. He made it 20 miles
before he couldn't hold himself up anymore.
On the radio they asked an officer
how he managed to hold on for so long.
He paused and you could almost
hear him shaking his head before he said,
"For dear life."

Terrible Men

Me and this dude talk shit on the corner. He says my dick is so big it got its own zip code. He says my dick is so big Jimi Hendrix couldn't chop it down with the edge of his hand. Me and this dude—this is my dude—and he is a fist. He says we drinking tonight, and we drink. My dude says get this shot and don't be a woman about it, a woman is something you love so much [you build an entire language of hatred around them]. He never calls a woman by her name, he says, (my, mine). He says, that's just how we roll [we built a structure. It is massive]. He says his dick is so big [it is the patriarchy]. He says ain't nothing more he loves than a woman. He says nothing more in this life he needs than a woman. He says a woman is something you need to punish for making you want them as much as you do. Bukowski kicked his wife during an interview. He says he loved women, he couldn't stop writing about them. My dude doesn't know about Bukowski. Can't talk right. Only speaks in all of his pain and the pain he causes others. He likes me because I'm the only one who'll listen to him; who won't call him a piece of shit even though he's a piece of shit. Sometimes he'll ask for a poem but won't go and read one himself. Sometimes he loves the poem and cries in my arms. Sometimes I tell him, *we're killing ourselves, my dude, we're killing us*. And sometimes I feel sympathy for the oppressor. Sometimes the bad man loves me like a brother. And, I confess, all I can do is hold it. That love which is another knot in both of our shoulders.

Doing Cocaine With You at 5am

You ask what I need right now, and what you mean
is water or another bump or the moon in a glass jar
and what I'm trying to say is your arms. Your arms.
There is a small puncture in the world,
I watch your fingers carefully
circling the lip. I don't want safety,
just hands and a map of this body.
I want to become more than memory.
I gather enough of myself
to say it, *maybe if you hold me,*
and you whisper back to me, yes. The empty space
inside of me collapses. We sit there staring at the table.
I watch you lean over and cut the next line.
When you tell me, it's ready,
I finally move, and ask for nothing else.

"*I am never home, but I am not lost…*"

— Sarah Maria Griffin

The Same Boy

What do I tell the woman I love
on the day she is leaving me?
That there are many homes
I have imagined, far and distant
from here. Further, still,
from the one we are leaving now.
Sometimes home is a mountain
and it rises and falls in breath,
a sleeping giant trapped
in the covers, that will not wake
until long after either one of us
are gone. More often, though,
it is a field. In the low-lying lands
where the rice stalks root out
of the water in praise.
There is my grandfather. Ankle deep
in the water. Pulling each straw
out of the mud. As alone
as I remember him
when the dementia took hold.

Do I say, all that is quiet and distant
in myself was born here. That I am
my father as he was his. And so
it goes, this thing that moves through
the years, as far back as the first grain
to ever have been yielded on our land.
Or maybe even further than that. A man
lost in foraging and always a mother
left to hold a boy in pieces. I wonder then,
if it is my own father who breaks the mold,
who tries so hard to be gentle and loving,
who often succeeds, but is nonetheless human.

Maybe we all try to be better men,
but are always doomed to keep producing
the same boy, instead. Maybe
the mountain was just some place
we had left when we could no longer
ignore the promise below. The wide

stretch of dirt and all that it could become.
The long plumes of green we must
tread through. All the tiring
and waking hours of the day.
And you see yourself growing old
here, and the wind picks up
and the wild stalk is singing
in your direction. And you imagine
a clearing. And you see
the house that sits
at the end of it.

Ain't Nothing Else to do in Texas but Drink Heavily and Regret All of Your Life Choices

I'm alone with too much whiskey
and nothing better to read
than the back of my palms.
The bartender pours me one last shot
and we toast to a better life than this.
My friends anchor themselves under my arms
and scream so loudly over the music.
It doesn't sound so much like drowning, but forgetting.
No one can see that my fingers are little match heads.
My boy says he wants to fight the men
on the other side of the bar. I tell him, don't.
I am always too ready and wanting of this.
Because I don't feel safe anywhere.
Because I am always having to be
everyone else's best memory of myself.
And there's always someone
who deserves to be the place where I put bad things.

I know I shouldn't but I can't stop thinking
about that girl who made me stop my car
and dance with her under a streetlight,
a long time ago, when cities were more familiar.
How I pressed my palm into her back
and she smiled before kissing me. When again,
I wonder, will this kind of boldness become me?
All I ever want is the wrong kind of brave.
Everybody says they lose themselves
in a moment like this. Me, I am never
more sure of where I need to be.

Kein/Muenchen

Nobody told me it snows in Germany during Winter. I brought all the wrong shoes, must have slipped on the ice seven times before eating it in the Botanical garden. There are several ways to get "got" in a city. The prime offense is to always be looking up. I couldn't help it though. I've never seen the street break form like this. Munich is so guttural and heavy on the tongue. The buildings are an impractical math. I am relearning shape. The city where I love is a grid, a digital timepiece: bending and folding: in and out of space. Here the streets are series of gears; the metal and the motor; all of it turning; the great wheel of time; it is breaking me; I am broken; I came here broken. I can say that now. There is enough time.

Today, being around people who speak a different language than me feels like less pressure. Bitte, bitte means please, but sounds so much like bitter. Kein, under my breath I repeat the word kein: I have no, I speak no, I am without.

A poet told me she wouldn't be able to translate one of the lines from my poem: "I love you in this city," and make it sound right. She said it wouldn't sound sincere. I didn't tell her, the person I wrote it for didn't think so either. I would have tried to make it sound like a joke. She wasn't getting my jokes. Instead she wrote one of my other lines on the wall: What else would it mean to be human if not a lost thing. I could have fell for her but I didn't. Maybe when we say love, we mean a safe place to fall apart.

I feel like Richie did that first night we took acid. Around 5am he said, "When is this shit gonna be over?" I'm listening to Junior tell me the same thing he told him, "Later."

You know how at some point, some asshole always ends up asking you the question, "If you were a superhero, what power would you have?" I hate that question. There's a superhero who talks to cities, but you don't want to explain who Jack Hawksmoor (God of the Cities) is. So you say what everyone else would say, I'd fly. I wish that someone would say, I'd spit medicine into my palms—or—I get stronger whenever I experience grief or loss. The more grief or loss I experience, the stronger I get. Don't make me sad. You wouldn't like me sad. Then maybe talking to cities wouldn't be such an outlying notion. Even today, in a place as cold and unfamiliar as Munich is this morning.

If I were a superhero I would talk to cities. Maybe to hear it say five more minutes, come back to bed. Some feral hound nuzzling it's way between us. I think of all the parts of me I am losing. How none of it makes me stronger, just different. I wonder if I'll ever be myself again. And if not, why would that be such a bad thing?

Munich, I am without. When I slipped on the ice nobody laughed. I'll get you for this, but you got me. You got me son.

Preface

During the summer of 2013 I packed up all my shit and drove home. That desert feels like it can go forever. It won't stop reading you. It knows you better than you do. You think you might have locked some stuff away but that road is open. Those maps are small, Texas is big. I wondered if I wasn't making some kind of huge mistake. All I wanted to do was go back to being the person I was when I left the first time. But you don't go home to remember who you are. You go home to reconcile with who you are becoming. The seasons of you are swift and forgiving. We are less so.

Antidepressants

If I ever receive a letter from my younger self asking,
what is it like to be older now? I'd write back—
Two words. More pills.

Why are so many bad decisions pleasurable.
Who is there to blame for these things? Aren't we
to learn from mistakes? Who would set up this binary
of reward and punishment only to throw in
a whole bunch of immediate rewards that become
punishments in later life? Is someone fucking with us?

Whose body is this? Who switched things out
when I wasn't looking?

———

I'm trying to figure out how to mark the years—
by the shape of my body, my great loves
or my great barbers, my clothes, the tattoos, poems,

all these departures we make
to our former selves? Always feeling
like I'm having to grieve for someone
who gets left behind.

Maybe to be born away from your homeland
is to carry a sense of loss you'll be struggling
to understand your whole life. How many different
types there are to be born into.

———

I've been to the pharmacist four times this month
and I'm always feeling like I have to explain myself.
Maybe a quick, "Just trying to get healthy man"
or "I've had insurance for two years and only used it twice,
one day I said to myself, I'm going to see all the doctors!"

The last time I went in, I am handed the bottle
of antidepressants I promised a former love
I'd look into, years ago. I accept
many things about who I am.

That there is a sadness in my body. That I got to push
a little harder to get shit done. That I spend more time
hidden because every bit of self-care is erased
when I become visible and brown in the world.

———————

I question what kind of person I've become,
how much I'm willing to accept because I don't think
we'll ever be able to win. But everything outside the window
is louder than it was the day before. And has grown louder, since.

———————

This morning my homie tells me maybe it isn't loss
that I'm born into but possibility. Always on the verge
of arrival. An iteration of "what if."

Maybe it's both. Maybe I can hold
all these things at the same time.
All of the grief and possibilities.

And, as he tells me, if that condition isn't Filipino,
I don't know what is.

———————

The first day I'm on antidepressants I wept in my chair
after popping that first pill. I thought it was because
I was ashamed, but it wasn't that. I could see
that away is what I've grown used to becoming.
But in the distance I could see it. I could see the way back.

The Nexus

In another story, we are not born as goodbyes
to an older country but tremors of the last night's monsoon—
the wet discarded rinds pulled from an aging fruit tree bending
toward the small shock of light caning through the palms.
Here we are not men who question the God we were given.
We are the elements and filled with hunger. I am still dark.
And I am still not told that this is beautiful. Here, we are children laying
in the grass. Our bellies sick with sugar cane, the dead stalk strewn about
in tribute. Here we are again, in the same field,
as grown men, who never learned their lesson. Maybe we understand our
parents better. Maybe we finally love them in the ways
they always deserved. In this story, I am stumbling drunk
down a street with two blown lamp posts. Even here,
I can't get most things right. When you catch up to me
I am dizzy against the wall struggling to take a piss.
Kuya, you tell me, *tabi tabi po*. Your voice filled with worry,
reminding me that we still owe pittance to all of our gods,
even those that are small and trade in mischief.
From here, you help me walk the rest of the way home.
And you listen to me tell you all that is troubling. Each of us
taking turns to wipe the sweat off our foreheads. Everything
is so quiet. Nothing but the sound of gravel scraping underfoot.

My College Roommate Calls Me on My Birthday.

All we do is talk about today. It gets hard to remember. 20 years ago we met each other—*can you believe that shit? 20* fucking years and I say, *remember that party we threw?* Can't remember where, don't remember what year, even the same places we used to go feel like they're somewhere else. I say, *remember that party?* When the needle was stuck at midnight and you could lick the bass in the air and swore it tasted like a woman's neck. I say, *remember that party?* We met 6am with nothing left in the tank and someone broke the sky open and you said this must be how the dead come back to life. I say, *remember that party?* And I'm thinking of the one where that OG breathing down cognac left us with best advice we were going to get. He said *you gonna ask these girls to dance and when they say no, move on and go, the one you want is the one who says yes.* And I say, *remember that party?* And I remember all of the ones I did not remember the day after. And I say, *remember that party?* And the gears of my knuckles turn ever so slightly. And I say, *remember that party?* You know the one where those two kids knuckled up right in front of us holding a fistful of each other's shirts inside of their palms. How we forgot to move out the way. Like we forgot we had legs. Like we didn't know one of them was about to be dead in the street in another two minutes. *We had the world once, didn't we?* Or is this something I tell myself when I want the better story. That in the end, no matter how much I moved, that world of ours moved further, faster. *I'm afraid I'm still trying to catch up.* I remember wasn't much written about the shooting. Just a small corner of the newspaper. The only person that looked scared was the shooter. The dead kid had a mouth on him. What a thing that must be? Even if your arrogance is foolish or unearned, it's power enough in the moment. A power enough to believe in. And power has a way of subsuming death. I wonder then, when the gun met his temple, where the power went. Did he hold firm his belief or did he die with that same loss and solitude that is all the reason some of us fear this moment. Did he die the way we never want to or can't stop thinking about. Or does everything open, or become more clear than it ever will be?

Sunday Night, Driving Over the Bay Bridge

She says there is a girl. And there is a field.
I do not know the measure of which,
or the distance between—only the weight
of memory, the city which is never permanent.

I do not recall, as easily, the first beautiful thing
I've experienced, but I know the first time
I was afraid, I remember when I understood
what it meant to hurt.

When she tells me all she wants to do
is protect that girl, I feel the little boy
who still clings to the hem of my shirt.

Maybe there is something for us in the city, today,
with its impossible permanence, it's walls that are written
and then written over. I'm thinking of something brave
and visible. My first beautiful memory, I'll say,
was a warm palm. It landed on my cheek.

How Do You Love a Gentrified City

Still you wait for the city
to hold you with a merciful hand
but didn't you know
a city is just like any god,
distant and aloof.

How can you be made so small
and expect to write the Filipino story big inside of this place?

And you say there is a pinhole, and inside, a mountain—
watch me now, watch me fit it all onto the whorl of my thumb.

Maybe tomorrow, they'll throw tear gas into the street and we will teach
them how to grieve properly.

You keep coming back. You're always told
there isn't a place. But you say, there will be one.

And you say, this is the city
where I found myself.
Where I've been punched in the face.
Where I've been punched in the face, again.
Where I was kicked once, in the face.
Where I lost my virginity.

                                    Where I fall in love, all of the time.

Could a home just be the place
where all your best stories live?
The ones that get told over good food or whiskey in a loud bar.

Where do we belong to more than memory?
A home that holds no capital.

The story of us
told in fifteen words:
we're still here. The heart
is both metaphor and material. This has kept us alive.

When I said sediment

                                              I meant sentiment

I make mud of it, homie

              watch what comes from the mud

Portrait of Steph Curry as Mac Dre on an Oakland Mural

"There is no there there" — Gertrude Stein

Maybe, Gertrude, this city was waiting to find
the right music. Maybe it's a little you
rendering language by the throat. But if there is
preciseness, the right tongue. Let it drop
a verse and reflect back on itself in disgust.
Let it be filthy and relished. Let it come at
the back end of a crossed up Australian
shook out of his sneakers. In a stadium
where the price of tickets will never go down.
In a city where the rent is always rising. When
the ball hits the bottom of the net
Steph Curry turns to the cameras, wearing
Mac Dre's mug on his face. Like a
secret. Like the very thing white folks
will trip over each other to understand.

"Can the subaltern speak?"

— Gayatri Chakravorty Spivak

Kamayan

My dad used to clean my chicken wings,
said I left too much meat on,
swiped off every last bit of flesh,
and threw it back on the plate
til the rattling sound wrung itself out
all over my American bones.
We used to joke about walking into Filipino homes
and there'd always be a big wooden spoon and fork
hanging on the wall. It is said
this is a sign of prosperity. How you tell people
that your home is blessed, and the people here live well.
My grandmother never stopped eating with her hands.
She'd sweep the rice into the crown of her fingers
and hold it upright for just a second of prayer
before driving it through her lips. It was the Spanish
who gave us utensils. Because only a colonizer
believes propriety is the same as liberation,
that they can walk into your house
and claim everything for themselves
because they remembered to take off their shoes.
Sometimes I catch my dad scooping the food
off the plate with his hands. Some momentary lapse
or glitch in the programming.
No shame to precede it, only a linger
over the last bits of rice clinging to his fingers,
the sauce hanging right off the tips

Murder on Murder Blinks

"I don't care if I burn in hell, for as long as the people I serve live in paradise."
— Joseph Duterte

The block breaks and bares the body
of a man. In certain parts of a city
they say birth means the same as dying.

At the point of impact, a standard bullet
creates only a small hole. Underneath
the skin, the bullet works upon the muscle
and nerves, dives against the bone,
creates a cavity that contracts as quickly
as it expands. The dying
happens on the inside.

He says he's a killing man. The president.
A punishing man. No one asks
if he really means this. In the city
where he was once mayor, there are people
who say they're no longer afraid
to walk the streets at night. Everything
has a cost. What are you willing to accept?

Someone must save this country from itself,
they say, the people deserve safety.

Every person deserves safety. But who's people
when we say this?

Aren't drugs about forgetting? To put a name in place
of hunger. Unthread the different needs of the body:
the need to sleep, the need to be touched, the need
to demand the justice that never comes. To forget
that home is always impermanent and cities offer you
no place to root. To forget the farms they grew up on
now generate profit for people they'll never meet.
The act of losing land becomes a condition
of our bodies. Nothing for us
is ever lost, only taken.

90

They say the people of the Philippines' greatest asset
is their ability to smile in the face of adversity, to live
the fullness of life through all of its challenges. How we afflict
ourselves with the benevolence of suffering. What is it
you see when you watch us
dancing inside the ruins of a typhoon?

Where are we supposed to put this pain? In the provinces
they sometimes craft their own guns from scrap metal
and spare parts. If every artist creates from a place
of loving, what is it to be a shaper of guns?
How do you name a passion that forges this kind
of talent? What do we do with all the dead it makes?

Only when the bleeding begins within,
do you start to bleed without. When blood meets
the air, isn't that a kind of holy water?

How does one extinguish
a bullet? How do you
put out a fire like that?

Notes on Maps

7,000 miles between Manila and San Francisco.
14 hours West to East
12 hours East to West
The planet spins counterclockwise
Pulling the atmosphere along with it
This is counterintuitive, to move into the spin
Should serve to shorten the distance traveled
Movement occurs on both sides of the line
But to fly back home is to fly against the Earth, itself
Between these two points the only thing that ever increases
Is time. Only memory. The story told.
The story in our own hands. That is time reclaimed.
Everything we can remember is unbeholden to distance.

Landfall, Home

Start with a dancer in pirouette. We say form, but it is the line.
What is pulled from the bottom of the feet, carrying into two arms
stretched and holding in the middle. This is a prayer's symmetry.
To the gods we rise and fall against. What reaches the sky
and comes crashing back to earth again, always dreaming
of higher ground.

Think of a spin that hungers. Speed as a living mechanism.
This is a typhoon. It eats the air and opens a million palms
clamoring for the first solid object to come crashing along it's fingers.
Maybe what it desires is intimacy. To understand human the way
we force ourselves to understand human. As a function of our mortality.

When the old myths talk about the destructive nature of the pantheon,
I don't recall if there were any stories of the ones who looked upon
the people below and thought it better
to move out of the way.

The people are resilient because they are resilient. There is a god
we deserve, into whose hands we can find our hands.

I often think they will never see us. Even the ones
we've built with our hearts. That all they would know
is how to lumber about with no regard
for everything it breaks below.

The gods who will look upon the splinters. The many dead and dying.
And think upon only an itch inside of their throats.

I see only gods in physical form, some unstoppable force or
bickering politicians on Olympus. I would want to say,
this is what a god means and it will fail you.

I am one of my people. Who do not say resilient
but what we leave is in God's hands. Who see the god in the sky
is only the mirror to the God that lives in the furthest point inside.

This is how my mother prays;
what I was taught in the home and not in the church.
How to hold power in the word. I spoke this over
every novena, every thumb running my mother's rosary.

I learned when you speak, you speak from the inside of you
and not from anything without.

Inside, is an entire line of us,
the beautiful ways in which we survive
we were born of the water and oftentimes
we will die inside of there, too.

I do not question if we are worthy of God
but I often wonder when it is
we will receive the god
who is worthy of us.

Am I a reliable narrator?   Does it matter?
Am I a reliable narrator?   Does it matter?
Am I a reliable narrator?   Does it matter?
Am I a reliable narrator?   Does it matter?

Am I a reliable narrator?   Does it matter?
Am I a reliable narrator?   Does it matter?
Am I a reliable narrator?   Does it matter?
Am I a reliable narrator?   Does it matter?

Am I a reliable narrator?   Does it matter?
Am I a reliable narrator?   Does it matter?
Am I a reliable narrator?   Does it matter?
Am I a reliable narrator?   Does it matter?

"They Sleep, We Live"

Preface

When I was twelve years old, I ended up at the same school as my older cousin. His crew rolled through campus about twelve deep, each of them bludgeoning out their bony chests to imagine the greater men they believed they'd grow into. When they hit me I gave them nothing to react to, as if holding it down might keep it all from breaking apart. They never told me to leave. I kept coming back, because I started believing I had nowhere else to go. Every night I prayed to God I'd wake up to a different life, and I wondered if I continued to shape it, if I made the world where I wanted to go, God would send me there. And each night passed, and each morning I was still here, and each day there was another me that walked alongside. This other me, who carries none of my faults and lives all my desires. I do not know why I have never let go of him, that I still continue to tell myself his story. All this in my hands and I still can't make him freer. I don't know how to reimagine the borders, or build a world better than this one. All I have is another me who survives it better. There is a flaw, though. Every time I've tried to tell this story I thought it was about the moment when everything started to fall apart. You see, all my life I've been looking for what has been trying to break me, but this story I've told you right now, is the one about how I've never been broken.

Four on the Floor

Can't get right with this wanting body.
The accumulating years, and my joints,
fuck these joints, and this back,
fuck this back is putting in work.
What a thing it must be
to have carried me this far.

Tired of people watching me slip to hunger so easy.
The mouth wants and is wanting. And I am trying
to learn this body again. Not just the weight
but my stride, how to get from one mile
to the next. Maybe it's true. Been thinking
maybe God wants me back. Been trying to explain
to everyone I ain't been gone. I'm always looking for holy.
I still say, *Amen*. There is enough in this life that deserves praise.
The blood moves through me, *Amen*.
My hips can still find the beat
and this face is still pretty, *Amen*.
There is good labor in this body. There is good work
being done. I know it works correctly. One day
someone is gonna prove me right. Someone is gonna
make a believer out of me. *Amen*.

I've done things to this body. Oh I've done some things.
Sometimes a sleepless night ain't nothing but the muscle memory.
I remember a lot less these days. More than the body is willing
to forget. These feet they want to move all of the time.
But here I am slogging through all this concrete.
I don't deserve this much rhythm.
These fresh ass dance moves belong
on more courageous hips. There are dance floors
all across this city with blissfully unaware white folks
swaying from all of their extremities. Taking up all the space.
Maybe I'll show them how the heart becomes
a metronome, that this is where you lead the body,
where you count time with your tongue,
where all the extra needs to go.
Put a little shimmy on it.
I don't know if this city can handle people
who look like me looking free.

Or what our free becomes in this space.
I ain't weary of what I'm holding here,
just protective. Unsure at times of how to hold this
and myself in the right measures.

Maybe I have everything to give up to this world right now.
The ache in my goodbyes, every last bit
of good cartilage and tendon,
the soles of my shoes.
Maybe when I shake
all my prayers are answered
and I get to be back in the world
with everyone else.
Maybe every first kiss don't have to feel
like finding land, again.
And the body I hold
is a body to believe in.
How it's a certain thunder.
Ain't nothing broken here,
just beat up a little.
It'll be alright, though.
It still floats, something pretty.
When it calls the roots of me come electric.
I'll be out the office, then.
Check my outgoing message.
It says, be back later,
we out here cooking.

Departures

I found a Betamax video tape a little while back that had my seventh birthday recorded on it, it's an hour of me and my cousins playing in the backyard. I took it to this shop in the city to get it transferred to file, but the tape was so old we they couldn't get the sound to encrypt. It's a silent movie, now, a meditation on the purity of play, a kinetic study, a glimpse of what it might look like to live without the context of the world, its history and present realities. It is, what I imagine, what free could be.

It is hard adjusting to seeing all of us getting older. In a lot of ways I'm still there on that tape, I am still running with my cousins. A little while ago we buried the youngest one of us. I don't think any of us could make sense that the first one of us to go would be the last of us born in this country.

Ate's husband gets on the mic during the funeral and he says that there's no way around this, that this one hurts. And he says, *grief is the price we pay for love*. And I look at this body of grief, and for once I choose to pay.

I am not afraid of my sadness or the cruel limits of the American imagination, which regards me less as alive, but within a perpetual state of dying. This body has always been an extraordinary gate of departure. I am made whole by all that leaves, but never truly leaves. I am made a living thing.

Greater Joy

How little there is to know of the body, that we would emerge
from the water, never a complete new—there, inside

a facsimile of older grief.

They say that the body inherits memory. Maybe
it is just the newer pain that learns to understand us
through us. Trauma as a wire through the generations.

"We are not alone in this," I repeat
then inhale. Each flush of air
sketching in my mind all the parts of me
that will remain hidden. This is a kind
of practice in faith, I tell myself.

On the day the coroner holds
my dead heart in his hands, what will we call it?
Out-of-commission parts? A collapsed engine?

What becomes of the well of ideas, the great
imagination, every bit of touch that ignites
and remains, still? Where does this go?

I want to believe that joy is inherited, too. Wouldn't they want
us to have this, as well? Doesn't everyone you love
deserve the entirety of you? Some day I'm gonna get gone
from here. Some day you will. I grieve for you, already.
But I believe that grief is an honest gift. It is how you learn
to hold the whole of a person. So much of loss
counted in the absence.

There is nothing missing, your fullness overwhelms me.
The rich and varied life of a person,
all of its requisite pleasure and madness.

Maybe we learn to live with losing,
make a world that loves us and our pain
in equal measure. In there is a greater joy,
I must believe it is one as equal
to the weight of our living.

"... where the rivers of weather
and the charred ghosts of old melodies
converge to flood my land
and sustain the one thicket
of memory that calls for me
to come and sit
among the tall canes"

— Garret Hongo

ASIDES

(p. 13)

Joe Bataan, a Black and Filipino gangster from Spanish Harlem who sang Latin Soul music. The single "Rap-O Clap-O" came out in 1979 and was released before the Sugarhill Gang's "Rapper's Delight."

(p. 15, Preface)

My cousin, Sam, was part of Nitelime Productions. Filipino DJ crew names almost never made reference to race, opting, instead, for a more disco and technology influenced branding.

(p. 18, A Song Reterritorializes)

Sampled tracks:
"Come Back to Me" (from *Rhythm Nation 1814*, 1989) Janet Jackson,
"Don't Walk Away" (from *Jade to the Max*, 1992) Jade,
"Stay" (from *Forever My Lady*, 1991) Jodeci,
"Come Go With Me" (from *Teddy*, 1979) Teddy Pendergrass,
"If Only You Knew" (from *I'm in Love Again*, 1983) Patti Labelle

(p. 23, Tesseract)

The tesseract is a four dimensional analogue of a cube, it holds it the way the 3rd can hold the 2nd in the palm of its hand. Though the first human bones in the Philippines were found 67,000 years ago, a recent discovery of stone tools and a cache of butchered rhino bones points to evidence of human activity on the islands dating back 700,000 years.

(p. 41)

I met Christine while we were both in college and performing with the Filipino comedy troupe, Tongue in a Mood, at the iconic Bindlestiff Studio. She wrote an incredible book about the relationship between post WWII Fil/Fil-ams and popular music called "Tropical Renditions" from which I pull this quote.

(p. 28, The Faith Healer)

Faith healers in my mother's part of the country are commonly known as *babaylan*, though this can vary by region. To quote Professor Leny Strobel, they serve the community as a "folk therapist, wisdom keeper, and philosopher." Though the role of *babaylan* is commonly associated with women, in some cases they can also be men.

(p. 36, Coded Language)

In 1961 Nat King Cole was the first international artist invited to perform at Araneta Coliseum (American musical artists became popular in the Philippines as the result of the numerous US military bases throughout the country). At the time, it was created to be one of the largest dome stadiums in the world, signaling the Philippines' entrance onto the economic world stage.

(p. 43, Preface)

As bad as we were at breakin', my little brother actually became good at it. He was a pop-locker, joined up with one of the best b-boy crews in our city, Rock4ce, when he was 13 and four years later they won Battle of the Year out in Germany (the last American b-boy crew to do it). Because of that he's been traveling the world for much of his adult life.

(p. 46, Into the Empty Field)

Fremont, California used to primarily be an agricultural community consisting of five separate townships. The introduction of a Ford auto plant (which is now home to Tesla) and the burgeoning tech industry in Silicon Valley spurred a development boom in the area and transformed acres of farmland into a modern suburb.

(p. 77, Antidepressants)

"maybe it isn't loss that you're born into but possibility. Always on the verge of arrival. An iteration of 'what if'" and "if that condition isn't Filipino, I don't know what is." credited to Patrick Rosal, who left that as a response to one of my Facebook status updates.

(p. 79, The Nexus)

My family went back to the Philippines in 1998, one of my *titos* was on his deathbed and his leg was swollen up, badly. Someone told my little brother that he took a piss in the street and didn't say "excuse me." You're supposed to do that because you might end up pissing on a *duende*'s home and if you don't excuse yourself you'll anger them and they will curse you.

(p. 82, How Do You Love a Gentrified City?)

There's a poem by Virginia Cerenio, she wrote in 1988 when she was working as a housing advocate in the South of Market district in SF. And in it she's talking to a redevelopment staffer, who says "'for the next twenty years, we are planning / the life of this place,'" and the poet wonders "where will they go, the families planting children like rice seedlings?" The Filipino population in the SoMa has decreased nearly three quarters from its peak over time. It's been over 30 years since she wrote the poem.

(p. 97)

A bartender at this spot I frequent, Demitria, put me onto this local electronic music podcast when I told her I wanted to start listening to house and drum 'n' bass again. Nackt had a couple of sessions on there and I really liked what he was doing. It felt soulful, like every moment of it was filled with intention. I picked up DJing over the last few years, and I know when I listen to people like him how wide of a chasm there is with where I'm at and where someone like him was—that you can feel every bit of the DJ throughout the music they're playing. The words "They Sleep, We Live" were tattooed on his arms; according to Demitria he got that from the John Carpenter movie *They Live* and turned it into a kind-of motto referencing the rave/club/dj life. Unfortunately he passed away in the Ghost Ship fire in Oakland in 2016. https://soundcloud.com/nacktmusic

ACKNOWLEDGMENTS

Thank you to the entire crew at Omnidawn, especially Rusty Morrison, for believing in me and helping my work find a new home.

Thank you to the editors of these magazines and journals where some of these poems first appeared (*World Literature Today, Muzzle Magazine, East Bay Review, Arroyo Literary Review, Mission and Tenth, BOAAT Journal, Laurel Review*) and the curators who featured some of these poems in their exhibitions at these galleries (Center for Art & Thought, Arc Gallery & Studios, Southern Exposure, Studio 110)

Thank you to Oliver Wang, whose book *Legions of Boom* helped connect me back to a history that informs so much of this book. Thank you to the multitude of Pilipinx writers and artists who are out there helping shape and transform the narratives of our community.

For all of your inspiration, your friendship, your support in helping this book come together, and for holding me up—thank you to Brynn Saito, Patrick Rosal, Kat Evasco, Jaz Sufi, Mike McGee, Mark Fabionar, Dara Del Rosario, Kimberley Arteche, Michelle Lin, Kazumi Chin, Anthony R. Miller, Natalie Ashodian, Derrick Brown, Anis Mojgani, my New Shit Show team who helped me write a bunch of these poems (Cam Awkward Rich, Jelal Huyler, Danez Smith, Joshua Merchant, Tatyana Brown, Sam Sax), Truong Tran, Barbara Jane Reyes, Sonya Renee, Christine No, Dan Lau, Jordan Ranft, Kay Nillson, Toaster, Brennan DeFrisco, Brandon Melendez, Nazelah Jamison, Maureen Benson, Puzzle, Lora Straub, Jaime Jacinto, Shirley Ancheta, Nancy Hom, and all the OGs that laid the foundation for us to work in.

Thank you to my Kearny Street Workshop family and this beautiful community I get to be a part of. Thanks to the Asian Pacific Islander Cultural Center of San Francisco, Bindlestiff Studio, SoMa Pilipinas, Z Space, Poetic Theater, San Jose Poetry Center, Arc Gallery & Studios, Chinese Culture Center and Manilatown Heritage Foundation.

Thank you to Sarah Gambito, Joseph Legaspi, Cathy Che, and all my Kundiman folks for bringing this community into my life and keeping it there.

Thanks to my boys 'til the end, Jaylee Alde and Mesej.

Thank you to every Pilipinx DJ for putting us on the dance floor.

And to my family, thank you for being my source of strength, for loving me unconditionally, and for never giving up on me.

Jason Bayani is the author of *Amulet* (Write Bloody Publishing, 2013). He's an MFA graduate from Saint Mary's College of California, a Kundiman fellow, and works as the Artistic Director for Kearny Street Workshop. Jason performs regularly around the country and recently debuted his solo theater show, "Locus of Control" in 2016.

Locus
Jason Bayani

Cover art: Rea Lynn de Guzman, "Flashback," 2018.
Image transfer on synthetic organza, 13" x 17"

Cover and interior set in Optima LT Std and Joanna MT Std

Cover and interior design by Gillian Olivia Blythe Hamel

Offset printed in the United States
by Sheridan Books, Chelsea, Michigan
On 55# Glatfelter B19 Antique
Acid Free Archival Quality Recycled Paper

Publication of this book was made possible in part by gifts from:
Mary Mackey
Francesca Bell
Katherine & John Gravendyk, in honor of Hillary Gravendyk
The New Place Fund

Omnidawn Publishing
Oakland, California
Staff and Volunteers, 2018–2019

Rusty Morrison & Ken Keegan, senior editors & co-publishers
Gillian Olivia Blythe Hamel, senior poetry editor & editor, *OmniVerse*
Trisha Peck, managing editor & program director
Cassandra Smith, poetry editor & book designer
Sharon Zetter, poetry editor and book designer
Liza Flum, poetry editor
Avren Keating, poetry editor & fiction editor
Juliana Paslay, fiction editor
Gail Aronson, fiction editor
SD Sumner, copyeditor
Emily Alexander, marketing manager
Lucy Burns, marketing assistant
Anna Morrison, marketing and editorial assistant
Terry A. Taplin, marketing assistant, social media
Caeden Dudley, editorial production assistant
Hiba Mohammadi, marketing assistant